Amersham

in old picture postcards

by
Colin J. Seabright

European Library - Zaltbommel/Netherlands MCMLXXXIV

GB   ISBN 90 288 2775 7

European Library in Zaltbommel/Netherlands publishes among other things the following series:

IN OLD PICTURE POSTCARDS *is a series of books which sets out to show what a particular place looked like and what life was like in Victorian and Edwardian times. A book about virtually every town in the United Kingdom is to be published in this series. By the end of this year about 175 different volumes will have appeared. 1,250 books have already been published devoted to the Netherlands with the title* **In oude ansichten.** *In Germany, Austria and Switzerland 500, 60 and 15 books have been published as* **In alten Ansichten;** *in France by the name* **En cartes postales anciennes** *and in Belgium as* **En cartes postales anciennes** *and/or* **In oude prentkaarten** *150 respectively 400 volumes have been published.*

For further particulars about published or forthcoming books, apply to your bookseller or direct to the publisher.

This edition has been printed and bound by Grafisch Bedrijf De Steigerpoort in Zaltbommel/Netherlands.

INTRODUCTION

Amersham, a country town in the Chiltern Hills of Buckinghamshire about 25 miles north-west of London, consists of two separate communities: the unspoilt 'Old Town' with its High Street described as one of England's finest and best-preserved examples of a mediaeval street, situated in the valley of the River Misbourne; and Amersham on the Hill, pure 'Metroland', a creation of the railway age, on the crest of the hill to the North. This book of postcards, all published between about 1895 and 1930, also covers Little Chalfont, another twentieth century product of the railway, and Chesham Bois, of ancient origins but predominantly a high-class modern residential district. Both are on the area of high ground between the Misbourne and Chess valleys, and now considered part of the overall Amersham.

A stone plaque erected by the Amersham Society on the side of the Market Hall sums up the town's history: 'In Saxon times the town was called Agmondesham. The Domesday Book of 1086 records it as Elmodesham with 3 watermills in use along the banks of the Misbourne. In the year 1200 King John granted Amersham the right to hold a market and a fair every year forever. Amersham was a borough for several centuries returning 2 members of parliament for periods between 1300 and 1832. Amersham was an active centre of Dissent from the 11th century onwards and some inhabitants suffered martyrdom. During the Civil War Amersham strongly adhered to the Parliamentary cause, and Oliver Cromwell's wife lived here. In the 17th century Amersham was the home of prominent Quakers who suffered great persecution. Amersham was renowned at the end of the 18th century as a centre of the black lace industry.' All this, of course applies to the 'Old Town' of Amersham, where the Misbourne still worked two of its mills until the beginning of this century. Its wide High Street and Broadway formed part of the main route from Aylesbury to London, and the demands of the passing traffic were met by many coaching inns set among a mixture of houses and cottages representing several periods and styles of architecture. The traditional Chiltern building materials, rough-hewn timber and split or knapped flints were used in the earliest buildings, the roofs thatched with local straw. These were gradually superceded by the bricks and roof-tiles produced locally from the early sixteenth century, and many houses were rebuilt or just re-fronted as fashions changed, particularly in the eighteenth century, so that outward appearances often hide their real age. In the middle of the nineteenth century there was a proposal to construct a railway line from Uxbridge to Aylesbury, following the Misbourne valley through Amersham as a natural gap through the Chilterns. This controversial scheme was supported by those who thought their business or trade would benefit, but was strongly opposed by the Drake family of Shardeloes, the main landowners of the area, because of the effect it would have on the view across their park. The opposition won the day, and their action saved Amersham town from the ravages of the twentieth century which inevitably centred on access by railway. Until the end of the nineteenth century, Amersham Common, which, together with Chesham Bois Common, stretched for miles along the ridge overlooking Amersham, was an area of open land with only a scattering of farms. On the other side of this, Chesham Bois, a village with its own long history, and also included in the Domesday Book, was more associated with neighbouring Chesham than with Amersham, from which it was separated by over a mile of common land. Chesham Bois never really developed into a village in the traditional sense, containing a number of separated houses and farms, but no village centre, and no pub!

When the railway eventually reached the district in the 1890's it was the Metropolitan Railway from London via Rickmansworth which traversed the ridge of Amersham Common on its route to Aylesbury. Stations were opened at 'Chalfont Road', some two miles to the East, and 'Amersham and Chesham Bois' (which later dropped the second part of its title) on the edge of the hill half a mile from Amersham town. Development started immediately around both stations, creating self-contained communities, known as Little Chalfont and Amersham on the Hill, with facilities to serve the needs of an increasing population.

Growth was accelerated in the twenties and thirties, with estates developed on land bought by the Metropolitan Railway and given the full Metroland publicity, and, with the transfer of the main Post Office and other businesses, Amersham on the Hill took over from the old town of Amersham as the commercial centre of the district. The traditional weekly market has been revived in recent years, but is now located in Amersham on the Hill, and the remaining shops in 'Old' Amersham, which has quite rightly become a tourist attraction, cater mainly for the visitors who come to see its historic buildings. As well as losing the bulk of its trade to its modern neighbour, the original town in the valley has also lost its name, for, in common parlance, 'Amersham' is now taken to mean Amersham on the Hill, necessitating the prefix 'Old' to define the real Amersham.

After the initial aerial view, the pictures in this volume are arranged in geographical sequence as a 'tour' of the area, starting from Shardeloes, and continuing through Old Amersham from the High Street, with detours into Rectory Hill and Whielden Street, to Broadway and Bury End. Amersham on the Hill is covered next, from Station Road through the shopping centre to Chesham Bois, followed by Little Chalfont.

The author gratefully acknowledges, as sources of historical detail, reference to many works about the area, including particularly the following:
A History of Amersham, by Goss, circa 1936.
The Book of Amersham, Birch, Barracuda 1976.
A History of Chesham Bois, Pike, 1976.
The Story of John Brazil, Archer, 1979.

High Street, Amersham from the Air.

1. This aerial view of the heart of Amersham, with its attractive jumble of roof-tops, shows the main features of the area around the Market Square as it was in the twenties. High Street enters the bottom of the picture and squeezes past the Market Hall, where the road widens again as Market Square, from which Church Street runs to the left in front of the Church and out of view. After the Square, the road width is even more severely reduced by the houses of Church Alley, where Whielden Street leads off to the right, then continues out of the town as Broadway. When Church Alley was demolished in 1939, so also were the cottages packed together behind it, and on their site the Garden of Remembrance, including the repositioned War Memorial, was dedicated in 1949.

Shardeloes, Amersham.

2. Shardeloes mansion was the home of the Drake family, who were the squires of Amersham, owned much of the town, and were responsible for many beneficial developments there. This house was built around 1760 after its predecessor, slightly higher up the hill, had been burnt down. The initial design, by Leadbetter, included four towers, but when a second architect, Robert Adam, was brought in to assist him, the frontage was changed to include the Portico and Corinthian columns which are the main features of the building. Drake family accounts record that half a million bricks were used in the construction of the mansion and the total cost was £19,000. During the Second World War Shardeloes was used as a maternity home, and later, after a period of neglect, was converted into luxury flats.

3. A view of the great park of Shardeloes, which was landscaped by Humphrey Repton, including the lake created by damming the little River Misbourne. This card was published over seventy years ago, but the scene is unchanged today. To the right of the mansion is the stable block, surmounted by an ornamental clock turret, and covering more ground than the house itself. There is evidence that this site was inhabited many centuries before the Drakes, for Roman remains were found a few years ago near the lake, including numerous roof and floor tiles and the foundations of flint walls.

Little Shardeloes, Amersham.

4. On entering Amersham from Shardeloes, almost the first house is Little Shardeloes, which was built in the late seventeenth century and extended in the eighteenth, and is believed to have been the dower house of the great manor. A high brick and flint wall, bearing the date 1688, separates the gardens from the High Street at the front of the house. This view, published in about 1905, shows the rear of the building, looking across its grounds which border on to The Platt, an ancient pathway behind the houses of the High Street, and a popular walk leading to Shardeloes Park.

The Old Town Mill, Amersham.

5. Opposite Little Shardeloes stands the old Town Mill, the first of the three Amersham mills powered by the Misbourne and recorded in the Domesday Book. This view, across the mill-pond, shows the back of the mill-house to the right of the actual mill. Both were built about 1600, but the house was extended later in the seventeenth century when a new wing was built in front, directly onto the High Street.

MILL STREAM AMERSHAM

6. This card of about 1900, and based on a painting, shows the downstream side of Town Mill, with the Misbourne flowing out under the bridge in Mill Lane. This mill was originally used for paper-making, but was later converted to grind corn, working until after the First World War. To the left of the mill-house can be seen the gables of Little Shardeloes House, behind its ancient garden wall. Although the flow of the river is greatly reduced today, this is still a popular paddling place for local children.

High Street, Amersham.

7. Next along the High Street, just the other side of Mill Lane, is the terrace of twelve small cottages known as Turpin's Row. Originally built in the seventeenth century as four houses, and believed to have included an inn, the cottages were, in the nineteenth century, the homes of working families, with the men employed by the Shardeloes estate or the brewery, and the women and children engaged either in lace-making or in straw-plaiting for the Luton hat industry. There is a local tradition that the Row is named after the infamous Dick Turpin, as the main road through Amersham was certainly subject to the attacks of highwaymen, but the truth is far less romantic, the property once belonged to a Thomas Turpin.

HIGH STREET, AMERSHAM.

8. A 1910 view of the other side of the High Street, including, between the trees, the courtyard wall of the ancient almshouses with its round-arched gateway. Beyond the trees, the tall square archway divides a seventeenth century building, believed to have been an inn, into two cottages. They are followed by another, still surviving inn, The Swan, dated 1671 but with modern bay windows and other additions. A little further on, hidden between the houses, Cherry Lane leads up to the hamlet of Woodrow, site of one of the old manors later amalgamated with that of Shardeloes under the Drake family.

The Almshouses, Amersham.

9. The plaque on the central gable of the almshouses tells that: 'Sir William Drake of Shardeloes in ye County of Bucks, Knight and Baronet. In the year of our Lord 1657 to the Glory of God and for the relief of six Poor Widdows well reputed in this Parish, Built six Almshouses, With all conveniences to them and A very good allowance for ever. At his owne Cost and Charge.' The houses are grouped around a small courtyard, two on each of three sides, with a brick wall including the gateway to the High Street on the fourth. Each house originally consisted of a bedsitting room, kitchen, and coal-cellar, and the allowance amounted to seven shillings per week, together with two loads of wood and coal annually, and a new gown every two years.

HIGH STREET, AMERSHAM

10. In this 1915 view from the centre of the High Street, the most prominent building is the twin-gabled public house, The Elephant and Castle, with modern restoration hiding its seventeenth century timbers. Next door is the original home of one of Amersham's most famous products, Brazil's sausages. The family butchers shop opened here before 1900, and after the First World War they started to make sausages and pies at the back of the shop. Business was so successful that a modern factory was erected in 1929 at the far end of the Broadway, expanding further as a household name until the retirement of the last member of the family in 1966.

HIGH STREET, AMERSHAM

2708

11. The country still came to town in about 1930, when this flock of sheep, under the control of the shepherd and his dog, encountered little traffic to impede its progress along the High Street. The first building on the left, Adams' shop, occupies the premises of the original Amersham Post Office, which had moved only a couple of years previously to a new building in Amersham on the Hill, and been replaced in the Old Town by a sub Post Office a few doors nearer to the Market Hall. The next building, Lloyds Bank, on the site of a flour mill, faces Elmodesham House, beyond which the Kings Arms, in its final 'Brewer's Tudor' splendour (see card 13), can be seen over the parked cars.

HIGH STREET AMERSHAM.

12. A 1900 view showing one of the earliest pedestrian crossings, a stone causeway laid through the mud created by the horse-drawn traffic, to enable residents to cross the road. Next door to the Red Lion, an older building than its Georgian front suggests, is Gurney's butchers shop, a seventeenth century timber-framed building, with a tethering ring in the edge of the kerb to hold animals awaiting slaughter. On the other side of the road the Kings Arms dates from the sixteenth century, and the adjoining building, at the edge of the picture, was considered an outstanding example of fifteenth century architecture. Later taken over as an annexe to the Hotel, it still contains many original features.

HIGH STREET, AMERSHAM   2699.

13. By 1920 the frontage of the Kings Arms had been altered by the addition of surface timbers, and its gabled annexe by the removal of plaster, to give an overall Tudor appearance. This was further enhanced a few years later by the construction of more oversailing gables, using genuine old beams rescued from elsewhere. The three-storeyed building just beyond the Hotel is Elmodesham House, built in about 1700 as a grand private residence, used from 1829 to 1862 as a school for 'the sons of liberal gentlemen', and since 1931 the home of Amersham Rural District Council and their successors, Chiltern District Council.

TOWN HALL, AMERSHAM.

14. Apparently painted on a very wet day in about 1900, this is a closer view of the Market Hall, frequently, but wrongly, known as the Town Hall. It is surmounted by an open-sided wooden turret containing the original bell of 1682, which was rung to announce the weekly market, and a four-faced clock. It is recorded that the north face of the clock, which was visible over the roof-tops from Church Street, was obscured for several years, on the instructions of the Weller family, to prevent employees of their brewery from clockwatching outside the premises.

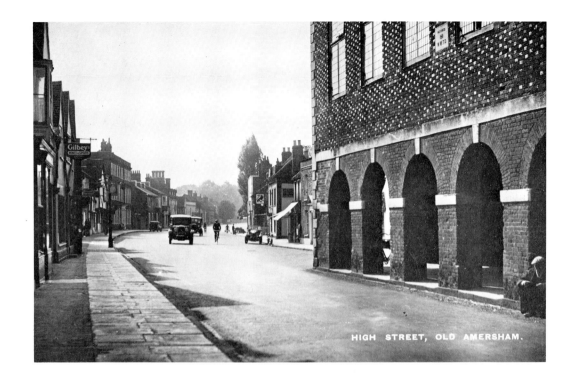

HIGH STREET, OLD AMERSHAM.

15. A 1930 view of the length of the High Street looking back along the side of the Market Hall, which shows the chequered brickwork of the upper storey and the stone commemorating the restoration of the building in 1911 by W.W. Tyrwhitt-Drake of Shardeloes. Although the main structure was still sound, the roof had been neglected and the interior had suffered from the effects of the weather. There have been many requests for the demolition of the Market Hall to ease the flow of traffic, but these have been strongly resisted, and the intention to build an Amersham bypass some time in the next few years should permanently end such suggestions.

AMERSHAM. A GLIMPSE FROM THE TOWN HALL   82585

16. The area under the arches of the Market Hall, which was built by Sir William Drake in 1682, housed the market originally established by a charter of 1200. Although the market declined in the middle of the nineteenth century, the custom of ringing the bell at noon on market day (Tuesday), continued until 1940. The upstairs room was reached by a staircase beside the old lock-up, and, since the application of stricter fire regulations, by a second staircase, seen here in the north-west corner. The room originally served as a meeting-place for the local trade guilds and as a court room, and at one time housed the Parish School. In recent years it has catered for a variety of public meetings, functions and entertainments from art exhibitions to jumble sales.

The Square, Amersham.

17. A 1925 view of Market Square, when it still was an enclosed square, with Church Alley at one end and the Market Hall at the other, seen through the open arch of the Market Hall. The building in the centre of the picture, with the large upstairs windows, was the first home of Dr. Challoner's School, founded in 1624 as a free grammar school under the will of Robert Challoner, Rector of Amersham. It remained here until moved to larger premises on the hill, and the curved stone over the doorway still bears the legend 'Grammar School 1624'.

Amersham.

18. One of the most frequently pictured scenes in Amersham, this card shows the view into Church Street in the early 1900's. The house on the left hand corner, of fifteenth century origin, is one of the oldest in the town. The shop on the other side is part of a seventeenth century house, retaining its original brick-filled timber framing on the gabled end facing Church Street, but refaced with brick and plaster on the Market Square frontage. On the corner of the shop, behind the gas lamp, a sign directs traffic for the station and for Chesham and beyond into Church Street, which leads to Rectory Hill, at this date still the main way out of Amersham to the North.

Amersham (from Rectory Hill)

G Ward. 118.

19. This was the view in 1915 from a little way up Rectory Hill, still only a narrow lane sunken between high hedges despite its importance as the main road to Amersham on the Hill. Looking back over the centre of Amersham, the Church is the most obvious feature, but the adjacent brewery, main industry of the town, is hidden behind the tree trunk, the smoke from its chimneys drifting across the valley. Beside the telegraph pole, the top of the 1784 Baptist Chapel, with its glazed octagonal lantern, can be seen over the roof-tops of the High Street next to Elmodesham House. The scene is little changed today, apart from the intrusion of an unsightly tower block at the hospital on the far side of the town.

The Rectory, Amersham.

20. The Rectory, situated in a commanding position on the hill overlooking Amersham from the North, was built in 1735 for the Reverend Benjamin Robertshaw, on the site of the former Rectory which had become so dilapidated that the previous incumbent had been forced to live elsewhere. The well-house in the garden, which was probably built for the previous house, contained the original horse-operated mechanism for raising the water. The name of Tenter Field, below the Rectory, and the inclusion of cloth weavers in early parish registers suggest the presence of a cloth mill in the town, but no evidence has yet been found of its existence.

THE RECTORY WOOD, AMERSHAM.

21. Rectory Wood, also known as Parsonage Wood, covers the upper part of the hill overlooking Amersham, and although it is privately owned, the public have had free access to the paths through it for several generations. One of the many paths starts in Rectory Hill opposite the drive to the Rectory, from which this view was taken. At the beginning of the twentieth century, postcards were issued and used for special occasions as well as for general correspondence, and this one, over-printed with New Year Greetings, was post-marked at mid-day on 1st January 1908, and would have been delivered in London the same day.

Amersham Church

ET King. Photo

22. In 1771 the local Weller family took over the former Church Brewery which faces the Parish Church across the River Misbourne, and steadily built up the business, finally owning 142 public houses in the surrounding districts. For over a century, half the working population of Amersham was employed in the brewery, in the associated maltings, or in the distribution of its popular product, 'Weller's Entire'. On the other side of Church Street the firm housed its dray horses in a large block of stables, now used as the Church Rooms. In 1929 the whole business was sold to Benskins, who subsequently closed down the Amersham Brewery, causing much unemployment in the town.

The Willows, Amersham.

23. The Misbourne flows beside the Church and continues past this line of pollarded willows behind the houses on the north side of Broadway. On the other bank, beyond the path, is the flint wall of the cemetery, and ahead is a cottage erected in 1855 in conjunction with the gas-works, which are hidden by the trees. For this 1905 view, the photographer was standing on the bridge which connects the churchyard to the cemetery gates and to the field path up the hill to Rectory Wood. Leading to Amersham on the Hill, this walk is still popular today with its extensive views over the Old Town.

The Parish Church, Amersham.

24. One of the most distinctive features of Amersham Church, prominent in views from all around, is the tower with its stair turret capped by a small spire. This was added in 1888 when the tower, originally built in 1480, was rebuilt using flints excavated from the railway cutting at the top of the hill. The whole building was 'restored' in Victorian times, and in 1908, shortly after the publication of this card, the Drake family vault was restored to its former use as a chapel. The displaced coffins were then re-buried in the churchyard marked by some fifty small stones placed close together, giving rise to the story that the Drakes must have been buried standing up.

Photo

25. St. Mary's Church dates partly from the thirteenth century, with many additions and alterations in the fourteenth and fifteenth, including the raising of the floor level by some three feet to prevent flooding by the nearby river, which has resulted in some very short doorways. This interior view was published in about 1900, at which time the author of one county guide dismissed the Church as 'a large flint building without architectural interest' and another as 'chiefly of Tudor date, but uninteresting'. Both, however, went on to describe the large number of memorials, statues, and brasses, many of them to members of the Drake family, which are among the Church's most treasured possessions.

AMERSHAM - MARKET SQUARE.

26. This 1920 view shows the eastern end of the Market Hall including the blocked arch which forms one wall of the old town lock-up, with the town pump of 1785 outside. Opposite the entrance to Church Street is the Georgian portico over the main doorway of the Crown Hotel, supported on pillars made up, like barrels, from narrow sections of wood bound together. In recent years this was damaged so often by passing traffic that it had to be removed. In the left foreground is the frontage of King's chemists shop, which, as proclaimed by the projecting sign, was also the local printing works, where some of the earliest postcards of Amersham were produced.

The Crown Hotel Yard,
Amersham, Bucks.

F. Read,
Proprietor.

27. A view of the cobbled yard of the Crown Hotel, looking out under the carriage arch into Market Square, is here used as an advertisement. The back of the Hotel and its range of outbuildings round the yard date from the seventeenth century, but the street frontage was completely rebuilt after a serious fire. A coaching inn and post-house, it was at one time used as the Petty Sessional Court, until this transferred to the Market Hall. In the nineteenth century it also housed the local Inland Revenue Office, and more recently the yard has been used as a film set on more than one occasion.

The Broadway, Amersham.

28. Leaving Market Square, this first view into Broadway shows the junction of Whielden Street. On the left, beyond the buildings of Church Alley, fields border directly onto the road, indicating the extent of Amersham Town in this direction in 1900. On the corner an old milestone, giving the distances on the High Wycombe turnpike, stands outside the ironmonger's shop which features a neat row of hanging watering-cans and buckets, and uses garden trellis fixed to the brickwork to display more of its wares.

AMERSHAM UNION.

29. The workhouse of the Amersham Poor Law Union was built at the distant end of Whielden Street in 1838, and is pictured here some sixty years later. Designed by the famous Buckinghamshire-born architect, George Gilbert Scott, in the Tudor style, and built at a cost of £7,000 using the traditional local materials, brick and flint, it accommodated over three hundred inmates from the area between Beaconsfield and Chesham, and served its original purpose until the Second World War. The extended premises were then taken over by a hospital evacuated from London, and, with further post-war additions including a controversial tower block which dwarfs the surrounding buildings, it is now the Amersham General Hospital.

Amersham from the South.

30. Facing the Union building is this cornfield which extends over the Southern slope of the Misbourne valley with a wide view over Amersham. At the left-hand corner of the field stands the Friends' Meeting House, created in 1685 by the extension of a cottage in which groups of Quakers had gathered for many years previously. Local membership of the Meeting declined and the building was vacated in 1850, when the Wesleyans took over for a period, but it reverted to its original purpose from 1917.

31. A closer view of Amersham from the southern side, looking over the roof-tops of Whielden Street, photographed from the track which leads up over the fields to Coleshill. Behind the Church tower plumes of smoke from the brewery are rising in front of the Rectory, which is splendidly situated among the trees on the northern hill. Below Rectory Wood, Rectory Hill cuts diagonally across the slope, with the footpath to the station crossing the field to its right. Although modern development has covered the hillside further east, this view has remained largely unaltered.

32. Whielden Street runs into Amersham down the dry valley from the South and forms part of the road from High Wycombe, here pictured at the edge of the town in about 1915. The road is believed to derive its name from William de Whildene, a local landowner in the fourteenth century. From the opening of the Amersham Union, a little further out of the town, until about 1910, it was known as Union Street. It is a small portion of the 'Gout Road', the turnpike maintained by the wealthy Cecil family from their Hatfield home to connect with the main Bath Road, thus easing their frequent journeys to take the waters in an attempt to gain relief from that ailment.

Whielden, Amersham.

G.Ward. 117.

33. One of many cards produced by local photographer George Ward, who recorded life in Amersham from 1880 onwards, this shows part of Whielden Street looking towards the Broadway. The tall seventeenth century building with four dormer windows, bearing the name of Henry Fuller's Drapery Stores, known locally as 'The Emporium', had been used as the local workhouse until replaced by the Amersham Union building. The passageway beside Fuller's leads to the Griffin Hotel yard, and was used by the first local buses which were based there.

Amersham. *P. O. Chorley Wood West. Herts. 24 10 04* High Street.

34. Church Alley, the block of dwellings in this 1900 view, and which extended from Market Square to the Broadway, was demolished in 1939 to reduce traffic congestion at the junction with Whielden Street. In the later years of its life, one of the houses was used by a bakery, which also owned premises in the row behind, necessitating carrying all their raw products across the public path in between. At the corner stands one of the early street lamps using the product of the nearby Amersham Gasworks.

AMERSHAM, THE BROADWAY

73315

35. The Griffin Hotel in the Broadway is one of the old inns which were much in demand in the coaching era; the rear of the building is Elizabethan, but the front was 'modernised' in the late seventeenth century. With three storeys and an attic, it was one of the tallest residential buildings in the town. The Griffin was the site of the first petrol pump in Amersham and, in about 1922, saw the foundation of the Amersham Bus Company, which initially operated services from the inn to as far as Chesham, extending later to Uxbridge, Aylesbury and High Wycombe. As the buses were unable to pass through the archway to the cobbled courtyard at the back of the premises, they were forced to make a detour into Whielden Street and along a farm track.

36. Beyond Church Alley the road widens as Broadway in front of the former maltings, the building with tall solid-looking brick chimney-stacks, here converted into a terrace of cottages and a small shop. Originally built in the fifteenth century, the front portion was damaged by fire in 1890 and restored with new bricks, and the upper storey was later used as a restaurant for some forty years until well into the 1960's. Subsequent alterations have changed all the cottages to shops, but their new shop-fronts, with attractive bow windows, are in keeping with the style of the buildings. This view clearly shows the narrow passage which was all that separated the terraced cottages beyond the maltings from the back of the properties in Church Row.

The Genuine 15th Century Olde Malte Tea House, Broadway, Amersham

37. The north wing of the maltings, pictured here as the 'genuine 15th century Olde Malte Tea House', retains much of the ancient timber framing and some panels of the original wattle and daub wall linings. The owners of the restaurant, which enjoyed magnificent views to the Church and Rectory Wood on two sides, but overlooked the gas-works on the third, summarised the building's history in their advertisements: 'This delightful old world building was actually used for nearly 500 years for the brewing of beer. The monks of 1425 brewed for a generation, until Henry the Eighth dispersed them, sold the premises and kept the money. Later it came into the hands of the Wellers, the well-known local brewers, who used it for brewing until 1907.'

Broodway, Amersham

*You can just see the market clock tower. The
Crown is just opposite. This is the way we came in —*

38. Despite its position on one of the main routes from London to Aylesbury, Amersham was a
tranquil place at the end of the nineteenth century, and this picture, taken in early morning sunshine,
shows the Broadway almost deserted apart from the two girls with their modern-looking bicycle. The
buildings on the south side, including houses and a few small shops, built in a wide variety of styles
and sizes and at various periods, present an attractive vista, almost unaltered to this day. The twin-
gabled seventeenth century house was at one time used for the manufacture of Windsor chair legs, and
in more recent times was the popular 'Number Eleven' restaurant, named after its address, which has
since changed with the complete re-numbering of all the houses in Broadway.

Old Houses, Amersham.

London House Series. 1593.

39. The view east from the Broadway is dominated by the frontage of Broadway House, of Elizabethan origin, which, instead of facing across the street, looks along it towards the Market Hall and consequently projects well in front of its seventeenth century neighbours. Facing these houses, set well back from the road and extending to the banks of the Misbourne, stands the gas-works which has served Amersham since 1855; and beyond that the bus garage, built in the early thirties, some fifteen years after the publication of this card.

LONDON ROAD, AMERSHAM.

40. These cottages orginally marked the furthest extent of Amersham, since the remaining premises beyond here on the London Road formed a separate hamlet known as Bury End. The board on the first cottage bears the following notice directed to strangers entering the town: '24th June, 1811. The Magistrates acting for this Hundred have given peremptory orders to the Constables and other Peace Officers to Apprehend all common Beggars, Ballad Singers, and other Vagrants so that they may be dealt with according to the Law.'

THE BURY FARM, AMERSHAM.

41. Bury Farm, built in the middle of the sixteenth century, was the principle building of the old hamlet of Bury End. In 1666 it became the home of Mary Pennington, when her husband Isaac was imprisoned and deprived of his house at Chalfont St. Giles for his Quaker beliefs. It was here that her daughter Gulielma Springett met and was courted by William Penn, who was to become famous as the founder of Pennsylvania. By the side of Bury Farm, Gore Hill, which climbs to Coleshill and Beaconsfield, is the traditional location of a bloody battle between the Danes and the Saxons. Halfway up the hill, until demolished in 1964 for road widening, stood The Pest House, where sufferers from the plague were confined in isolation from the rest of the community in the seventeenth and eighteenth centuries.

42. This is the view back towards the Bury End of Amersham from the London Road, photographed in about 1900. To the right, over the wall, is the Bury Mill, and behind the hedge the Chequers Inn; ahead is a block of cottages which stood at the foot of Station Road. Bury Mill is thought to be one of those recorded in the Domesday Book, and was specifically mentioned in documents of 1504. It is the lowest of the Amersham mills on the Misbourne, and remained operational into this century, but has more recently been used as the Millstream restaurant, and is now a high-class fashion showroom. The tail-race of the mill flows under the bridge in the foreground, while the main river is crossed on the far side of the group of trees, which have long since given way to road widening.

The Missbourne, Amersham.

43. Below Amersham the Misbourne meanders through the pastures on its way to Chalfont St. Giles and Chalfont St. Peter, to which it was possible to skate in the hard winters of the last century. The origin of the river's name is Mease, the celtic word for a stream, and in Saxon times it was known as the Messebourne, but never as the Missbourne as on the title of this early card. The flow of the river has always been erratic, occasionally drying up altogether on the surface, flowing instead as an underground stream through the chalk, and there is a local tradition that its disappearance foretells a national disaster, as it did this century before both world wars.

Beechwoods, Amersham.

44. This was the view, in about 1915, from the slope below Amersham station, looking down the valley of Station Road towards the Old Town and the hills on the other side of the Misbourne. Originating as a farm track, Station Road was still only a minor road, but the residential development along it and the increased demands of traffic to and from the station led to its straightening and widening in 1929. It then took over from Rectory Hill as the main link between the two halves of Amersham. New building started immediately alongside the road (in progress at the right-hand edge of this picture) but later spread over the open fields, particularly on the left, where it eventually covered the crest of the hill, here crowned by Batchelor's Wood.

45. The new Amersham soon started to expand from its nucleus, the station, and this view shows part of Station Road, looking down from the railway bridge in about 1912. The first shop on the left was the drapery stores of the Misses Peck, who also published postcards, including several of the views used in this book, their later cards being issued as 'London House' series after the grand name given to their premises. At the other end of this short parade of shops stands the Bijou Hall, initially used for 'entertainments and dancing', then for a short period as the Playbox Cinema, in 1936 becoming the Amersham Repertory Theatre and finally the local Auction Rooms.

STATION ROAD, AMERSHAM.

46. With the arrival of the railway, the first new buildings of Amersham on the Hill were at the top of Station Road, adjacent to the Metropolitan Railway station, and included two hotels. In this view, taken from the up platform in about 1900, the Metropolitan Temperance Hotel, at the left and almost in the shadow of the railway bridge, faces the Station Hotel. All the pictured buildings still exist, although the Temperance Hotel, which served as unofficial dining-room to the first pupils of the nearby Grammar School, is now used as Council offices, and the Station Hotel has been considerably altered and renamed The Iron Horse. The first sub Post Office of Amersham 'Newtown' was established a few years later in Mrs. Neville's confectionery shop which opened in the other half of the Temperance Hotel building.

Dr. Challoner's Grammar School, Amersham.

47. In 1905, Doctor Challoner's Grammar School had outgrown its premises in Old Amersham and moved to a new site on the hill. This building, containing the Headmaster's house as well as assembly hall and classrooms for ninety pupils, was constructed by a local builder for a little over £5,000, on a six acre site on the main Amersham to Chesham road at the top of Station Road. Unlike the original school, the new one, opened in September 1905, took both boys and girls, and the building, pictured here very soon after the opening, still exists among the many modern additions. The school remained co-educational until 1962, when, with no room for further expansion here, the girls were transferred to a new school at Little Chalfont.

AMERSHAM, HILL AVENUE.

59456.

48. Hill Avenue, the main thoroughfare from the station to the centre of Amersham on the Hill, remained unsurfaced for the first thirty years, despite the growth of the modern shopping centre, and older residents still recall the necessity for gum-boots because of the pot-holes in the road. When this picture was taken, in about 1930, the new parade of shops, all resplendent with sunblinds, had not long been completed. Further commercial development gradually occupied almost all of Hill Avenue, but the pair of houses on the left of the picture remains today, sandwiched between parades of shops and part of the telephone exchange.

CHESHAM ROAD, AMERSHAM COMMON

49. The next few cards illustrate the early growth of the main shopping centre of Amersham on the Hill around Oakfield Corner and along Sycamore Road. This first, of about 1915, shows the view into Chesham Road from the side of the main cross-roads at Oakfield Corner, with the Doctor's surgery, one of the first few large houses built along from the Grammar School, facing the new parade of shops through the line of large oak trees at the roadside. There has been no further shop development in this direction, but more houses were built in the following years along the Chesham Road. This card, published by Misses Peck of Station Road, still uses the original name for the area; Amersham Common.

SYCAMORE ROAD, AMERSHAM COMMON.

50. Another card from Peck's series shows the view from the same corner looking into Sycamore Road, previously a country lane to Chesham Bois, showing the full extent of the development at this date, on one side of the road only, facing across the open fields to Woodside Farm. The pavement awning is over a branch of the International Stores, which had opened originally just around the corner in Chesham Road, but later moved into this, more popular part of the shopping centre, where it remained until about ten years ago. Past the shops on this side of the road was a large private house on whose orchard the Central Parade was to be built in the thirties, featuring, as did most suburban shopping centres of that period, branches of Boots and Sainsburys.

51. By the date of this card, postmarked 1924, shops had been built along the other side of Sycamore Road, though this development was in a more piecemeal way than the facing parade, with a mixture of separated single-storey shops and others with accommodation above. The former Kennards shop on the left-hand corner had now become the National Provincial and Union Bank, with Barclays Bank opposite, in premises it still occupies today. Similarly descendants of the estate agent, Mr. F.E. Howard, whose sales were advertised outside, still use the premises on the other corner.

Sycamore Road, Amersham

52. Further along Sycamore Road towards Chesham Bois, this isolated pair, still standing today among the more recent developments, marked the limit of the Amersham shopping centre for some years. More shops were then built on the other side of the road, together with the Regent Cinema of 1928, which was demolished in 1962 to make way for a supermarket. Behind the elm trees, which were to remain an Amersham landmark until the 1960's, stood St. Michael's Church and Hall and the Free Church, on sites which proved a goldmine when eventually sold for further shopping development.

Cross Roads, Chesham Bois.

Published by E & W Pape

53. Here Sycamore Road continues from the shopping centre, across the Rickmansworth Road at what is now known as Sycamore Corner, leading (left) to Chesham Bois, while Woodside Road runs ahead to Amersham Common and on to Little Chalfont. In 1932 the area around Woodside Road and extending to and beyond the railway line began to be developed as part of 'Metroland', with reasonably priced homes (semi-detached from £875), built by private contractors for the Metropolitan Railway Company.

CHESHAM BOIS' · AMERSHAM STATION · CAUTION DRIVE SLOWLY

GRIMSDELL'S LANE, AMERSHAM 2655

54. At the turn of the century, the only buildings in this part of Amersham, on the way to Chesham Bois, were the forge, on the right of Grimsdell's Lane, and the cottages behind it, which still stand at the corner of Short Way. When this picture was published, in about 1925, one side of the road was built up almost as far as the old 'Pheasant' Inn, and the first new houses were under construction on the other. The footpath, running off to the left between the trees at the corner of Sycamore Road and Grimsdell's Lane, still remains, a relic of the old tracks across the former Amersham Common. This path, like others in the area, cuts diagonally between the new residential roads, giving many of the houses triangular gardens.

The Common, Chesham Bois.   Pub by. E.&.W. East.

55. This view, published about 1910, from the edge of the Common near Heatherton House School, shows the junction of Copperkins Lane with the Chesham Road, then little more than a country lane (between the lines of posts), now the A416, a major link road between the M1 and M4 motorways. South Road leads away in the centre of the picture, with further houses facing Chesham Road to the right, behind which the rooftops of Lexham Gardens can be seen. These were among the earliest developments of the new Amersham, mainly smaller houses within easy reach of the station.

56. As well as scenic souvenirs, postcards used to be issued to record all sorts of local events, and to supplement the newspapers, which carried no illustrations. This card, published in November 1908, pictures the disastrous fire at Copperkins, Chesham Bois, with 'before' and 'after' views of the house, which stood at the beginning of Copperkins Lane. There has never been any satisfactory explanation for the name of the lane, which leads over the once open common-land (the continuation of Amersham and Chesham Bois Commons) to the next village, Hyde Heath.

Bois Avenue, Chesham Bois.

W.H.A
Photo Series. 729.

57. In the early years of this century, many superior residences were built in Chesham Bois for the company directors and bank managers who chose to live in rural comfort and commute daily to London by the Metropolitan Railway. In 1910, a Pullman service was introduced on the line from the City to Amersham and Aylesbury, providing additional comfort and the luxury of refreshments en route for those able to afford it. This housing development centred on the Copperkins Lane area, and the card shows Bois Avenue in about 1914, with detached houses already built on nearly every plot.

THE POND, CHESHAM BOIS

Published by Smith Bros., Chesham

58. The pond alongside the North Road edge of Chesham Bois Common, together with the many deeper hollows among the trees behind the girl in this 1900 view, was created by the extraction of clay for the local brickworks. The brick-making industry was established here in the seventeenth century, with kilns probably on the other side of the road, where the meadow behind the present Ken House Hotel was once known as Brick Kiln Field.

THE COMMON, CHESHAM BOIS. 3.

COLES, Watford.

59. Pictured in 1905, Chesham Bois Common was then mainly an expanse of close-cropped grass, with areas of bracken and gorse, particularly toward South Road, and a few mature trees in this avenue which shaded the Rectory garden. Natural seeding and regeneration, together with some planting in 1919, have greatly increased the area of trees and scrub, and the cricket pitch is now the only open space of any size. The forty acres of the present common, which is owned by the Lord of the Manor but leased to the Parish Council, is the relic of the original common land which extended for over two miles from the district now known as Amersham Common to the far end of Copperkins Lane.

BOIS COMMON,
CHESHAM

60. North Road marks, as its name suggests, the northern extremity of Chesham Bois Common, and when this card was published, about 1905, was already becoming a select residential road. In addition to the sixteenth century Manor Farm and its barn and several farm-workers' cottages, all of which had been converted into desirable homes, more large detached and semi-detached houses had been built on extensive plots with open views across the common.

61. The subject of this 1900 card is Manor Lodge, one of the historic properties in North Road, facing the common. It was originally a group of cottages for workers of the neighbouring Manor Farm, and was converted into a single residence in the nineteenth century. At the time of this card, the lands of Manor Farm, which covered the area between the common and Great Bois Wood, were undergoing development as large, well-spaced houses, and the principle residential road in the area, Long Park, is named after one of its fields.

The Rectory, Chesham Bois.

62. The Rectory is delightfully situated on Chesham Bois Common, close to the heart of the village, but some half mile from the Church. It was built in 1833 by the Duke of Bedford, patron of the living, when one of his relations was Rector; is in the same traditional style as his estate cottages at Chenies, and bears the family arms over the entrance. Pictured here at the turn of the century, the building remained the home of the Rectors of Chesham Bois until 1983, when a new house, more in keeping with the needs of the present-day incumbent, was built just the other side of the Church hall, which had been erected next to the Rectory stable-block in 1937.

Chesham Bois.

63. At the end of North Road, near the Rectory, a triangle of common is separated from the rest by the link road which cuts across to the corner of Chestnut Lane, and from which the delivery van is turning in this view of about 1910. This section of road was un-named until 1983, when, in order to give an address to the new Rectory being built there, the name Glebe Way was chosen for it. The magnificent elm trees on the triangle, which housed a large rookery, remained until only a few years ago when they fell victim to Dutch Elm disease.

Downash. Chesham Bois.

64. Downash, at the corner of Chestnut Lane, originally named Red Lion Road after the Inn at its far end, was built as the village school in 1846. The building, behind the tree in this view, is of local flint with a roof of Bangor slate, which had just become generally available with the improvements in transport. It included the home for the one schoolmistress and was built for £150. In 1894, when the new school was built in Bois Lane near the Parish Church, it was sold at auction for £385, since when it has been used as a private residence.

Anne's Corner, Chesham Bois.

65. This view, of about 1905, shows the approach to Chesham Bois village from the end of Sycamore Road. The cottages are the beginning of Bois Lane, which leads past Anne's Corner and continues to the Parish Church and the school, from which the two little girls are probably returning home. On the corner of the common opposite Anne's Corner stands a notice listing the byelaws for the maintenance of Chesham Bois Common, on the site which was later to carry the War Memorial.

ANNE'S CORNER
BOIS COMMON,
BUCKS.

66. Anne's Corner, this attractive block of three houses, built at the turn of the century in Tudor style, has given its name to the area which now forms the heart of Chesham Bois Village. In this 1910 view, the first house has a 'Let' sign in the window, and it is interesting to note that the publisher has obliterated the wording from the sign projecting from the corner, presumably to avoid giving a free advertisement to the estate agent. The right-hand end of the building soon became, and has remained, the Chesham Bois sub Post Office, facing a group of four cottages with added shop fronts which make up the village shopping centre.

67. Opposite Anne's Corner, on the edge of the common, and backed by a line of fir trees (which now dominate it), stands the village War Memorial. 'Erected to the memory of those of this parish who fell in the great war 1914-1918,' it lists, on the column, the names of the thirty-one villagers who died. On the plinth has since been added the Roll of Honour for the Second World War, a further nineteen names. Facing the common, in Bois Lane, the line of cottages dates from before 1900, one of them having a carved lintel bearing the name 'Sloe Cottage', after the fruit of the blackthorn which was widespread in the scrubland of this area.

68. This 1905 card shows a part of Bois Lane, the road to Chesham Bois Parish Church and on down the hill to Chesham Moor and to Chesham. Not long previously the lower part of the lane was still only a grassy track, but in 1888, when the Chesham branch railway was constructed, it was diverted to the newly built railway bridge and generally improved. Facing these cottages, which still remain, development soon took place on the other side of the road, including a corrugated-iron cottage which provided the first Postal service, but some of these houses have since been replaced.

Holloway Lane, Chesham Bois.

W.HA.1585

69. Holloway Lane, dropping steeply down from Chesham Bois into the Chess valley, forms part of a prehistoric trackway which ran from the Thames, via Beaconsfield, Coleshill and Amersham, to Ley Hill on the distant hills in this view. In the nineteenth century the 'hollow way' ran through a large area of woodland, but by 1925, the date of this picture, most of the trees had been displaced by the very large properties occupying the dip to the left of the road. Subsequent development on parts of their gardens and alongside the road have made this a popular residential area, but the lower half of the road, below the railway and down to the river, is still only a narrow lane, hardly suitable for modern traffic.

70. Adjacent to the Church, in Warren Meadow, stood the original Chesham Bois Manor House, built or possibly rebuilt in about 1213 by William du Bois. The village takes the second part of its name from his family rather than from the wooded nature of the countryside. The Manor House was demolished in 1812, and some of the materials and fittings were reused in the construction at that time of a new residence for the Weller family, the owners of Amersham Brewery, but the foundations remained near these houses beside the Church.

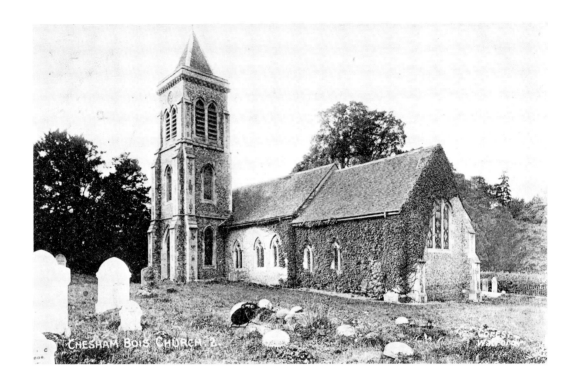

71. The Church of St. Leonard, Chesham Bois, is situated on the edge of the slope down to Chesham Moor, remote from the heart of the village it serves, having been built in 1216 as the family chapel for the manor-house which stood nearby. The present chancel is the original structure, the nave was added in the fourteenth century, and further extensions and alterations were carried out in Victorian times, including the tower, which was still fairly new when this picture was taken. For a long time Chesham Bois was only a chapelry dependant on the Parish Church of Chesham, becoming a parish in its own right at the beginning of the nineteenth century.

RAAN'S FARM, AMERSHAM COMMON.

72. The manor of Raans was one of some half a dozen which, between them, included the area of the present Amersham. Named after the holders of the estate in the twelfth to fourteenth centuries, de Rane or de Raan, it passed through many hands until, in 1619, it came into the possession of the Proby family. Raans Farm, which had been built in 1540, was then extended and the Proby arms displayed over the door. Despite some subsequent alterations much of the present building dates from this period. The farm's fields now form a breathing space between the developments of Amersham on the Hill and Little Chalfont, on the edge of the high ground overlooking the Chess valley.

73. This card, published in about 1915, shows some of the properties at Amersham Common, the small community half-way between Amersham and Little Chalfont which has retained the name of the original extensive tract of common-land. The three-wheeled car and the pedestrians are standing outside the sub Post Office, and the horse-drawn cart is at the end of the drive to the old Pineapple Inn, set back behind the field in which its sign stands. Beyond this are some old cottages and the barn of the historic Barkers Farm.

CHALFONT ROAD STATION.

74. On 8 July 1889 the extension of the Metropolitan Railway was opened to Chalfont Road (later renamed Chalfont and Latimer) and, via the single track twisting down the side of the Chess valley, to Chesham. The Chesham line became the branch when the main line was constructed to Amersham and Aylesbury three years later. This early picture shows the little buildings with the curved corrugated iron tops, protecting the ends of the subway connecting the platforms, which still stand today under the extended platform awnings.

BIRDS' EYE VIEW OF LITTLE CHALFONT

75. This early view of 'Little Chalfont', the name given to the district by one of the property developers shortly after the First World War, was taken from the Rickmansworth Road, and shows the station on the embankment together with the beginnings of the community which grew up around it. Until the arrival of the railway this was open country at the junction of the road to Chalfont St. Giles and Chalfont St. Peter (which gave the initial name Chalfont Road to the station) with the main road from Rickmansworth to Amersham, which here curves sharply under the railway behind the telegraph pole.

CORNER OF LITTLE CHALFONT

76. This card shows the first stage of development in Village Way, a private estate very close to Chalfont and Latimer station, from which the London business-man could travel to the City in the comfort of first-class for only £9 per quarter in 1930. These houses were built in the country cottage style which was popular in the outer parts of 'Metroland' at that period, some with thatched roofs, and, as they still do, they enjoyed complete seclusion, tucked away in a little hollow out of sight of the main road through the village, despite their nearness to it.